Real Life: Storytellers

Written by Sean Callery

Contents

Painting with Words

People have told stories all through history, to entertain or pass on important information. In the 1800s, the brothers Grimm became some of the first famous children's authors. They wrote **traditional** stories such as *Cinderella*, *The Frog Prince* and *Snow White*.

Grimm's Fairy Tales

Later, there were other well-known writers for children such as Rudyard Kipling, who wrote *The Jungle Book*, and C. S. Lewis, author of the *Chronicles of Narnia* books. These authors are probably more famous now than they were when they were alive. Their stories are available all around the world and have been told again as plays and films.

There are so many stories to choose from ...

Bringing the Page to Life

Becoming a famous children's author is not easy. You need to create stories with fresh ideas and characters and write in an exciting way. Some storytellers get their ideas from amazing things that happen in their lives. Others have incredible imaginations, which help them to create interesting characters. All great stories need an exciting **plot** with plenty of surprises.

A Love of Stories

The storytellers in this book are very successful children's authors. They have used their talent and experience to create wonderful characters, such as Harry Potter and Alex Rider, and fantastic stories such as *Matilda* and *War Horse*.

The Lion the Witch and the Wardrobe

Many of their books have been made into films.

J. K. Rowling and Anthony Horowitz started writing when they were very young. Roald Dahl and Michael Morpurgo came to it later in life. They have led very different lives but they all have something in common: they adored hearing and reading stories as children.

Roald Dahl

FACT FILE

- **Name:** Roald Dahl
- **Date of birth:** 13th September 1916
- **Nationality:** British, with Norwegian parents
- **Famous books include:** *James and the Giant Peach, Charlie and the Chocolate Factory* and *The BFG.*
- **Favourite author:** Ernest Hemingway
- **Liked:** chocolate, flying, photography and collecting furniture and paintings

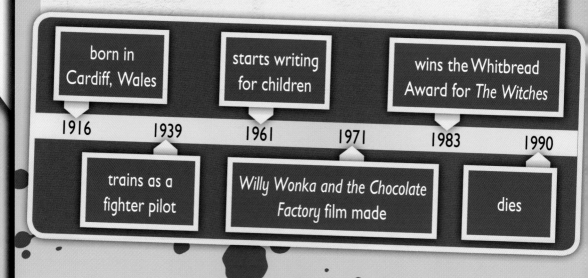

born in Cardiff, Wales

starts writing for children

wins the Whitbread Award for *The Witches*

1916   1939   1961   1971   1983   1990

trains as a fighter pilot

Willy Wonka and the Chocolate Factory film made

dies

A Hard Start

Roald Dahl is one of the most popular children's authors ever, selling millions of copies of his funny stories full of wacky characters. But there wasn't much to laugh at in his difficult childhood.

Roald's parents were from Norway, and named him after the Norwegian explorer, Roald Amundsen. His father died when Roald was three years old, and he was later sent away to boarding school where he was homesick and unhappy. The only thing he was really good at was sport.

Roald's school reports say that he wasn't a hard worker.

The unkindness of some adults at school influenced Roald's writing. The grown-ups in his stories are often stupid or cruel, and these 'baddies' always get punished!

Gobstoppers

Roald began getting into trouble at school. One school report complained he was lazy. Once he got told off for putting a dead mouse in a jar of **gobstoppers** in the local sweet shop. He and his friends called this "The Great Mouse Plot of 1924".

Seeking Adventure

After he finished school Roald could have gone to university, but he decided to travel and have adventures instead. He looked for jobs in faraway places. First, he worked for an oil company in Tanzania. Then, when the Second World War began, 23-year-old Roald joined the Royal Air Force (RAF).

Roald trained as a fighter pilot.

Bumpy Start

On his first mission, Roald was lucky to survive a crash-landing in the African desert. He escaped but was badly burned and left with a **permanent** limp. It was six months before he was able to fly again, but he went on to become a very successful pilot.

The Second World War (1939–45) was a battle between two groups of countries: the Allies (including the UK, USA and many other countries), and the Axis (including Germany, Italy and Japan). It was fought all around the world, on land, at sea and in the air.

Sky Writing

Roald was sent to Washington DC in 1942 as an air **attaché**, helping to find and pass on useful information – he was a sort of spy. He wrote a story in a magazine about his scary wartime crash-landing. It was a great success and Roald was asked to write more tales about the war.

Kid's Stuff

In 1953 Roald married an actress called Patricia Neal and they moved back to England. They went on to have five children and Roald loved making up long, funny bedtime stories for them. When he started to publish these, he stopped writing for adults.

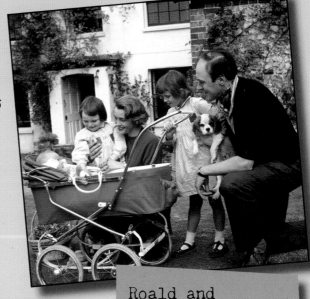

Roald and Patricia's marriage lasted for 30 years.

You have to keep things ticking along. And if you think a child is getting bored, you must think up something that jolts it back. Something that tickles.
Roald Dahl

Big Ideas from a Small Hut

From 1961, Roald created his children's books in a hut in his garden. He would sit in an armchair with his feet propped up on the desk and a rug over his legs. With a board resting on his knees, he scribbled ideas and stories in pencil on to lined paper.

Roald's old garden hut is now famous!

The hut was in an orchard, and its fruit trees gave him an idea for one of his early stories. Roald imagined what might happen if the fruits didn't stop growing. This was the inspiration for *James and the Giant Peach*. The book was a big success. Roald was on his way to being a very popular children's writer.

James meets six wacky insects during his time in the giant peach.

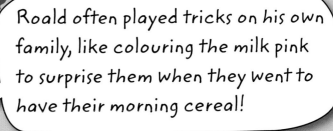

Roald often played tricks on his own family, like colouring the milk pink to surprise them when they went to have their morning cereal!

International Success

Over the following decades, Roald wrote more than 20 books of stories and poems. They sold millions of copies and were translated into 34 languages. Six of his books have been made into films, including *Matilda* (1996), *Charlie and the Chocolate Factory* (1971 and again in 2005) and *Fantastic Mr Fox* (2009).

Roald loved chocolate. He kept a ball made of chocolate wrappers on his desk. It was very heavy!

The Roald Dahl Museum has a snack shop called Café Twit.

Still Remembered

After his death in 1990, Roald was buried with his snooker cues, some chocolate and a set of the HB pencils he always wrote with. His name lives on through his stories and poems as well as through the Roald Dahl Museum and Roald Dahl's Marvellous Children's Charity, a charity that helps poor and sick children.

Michael Morpurgo

FACT FILE

- **Name:** Michael Morpurgo
- **Date of birth:** 5th October 1943
- **Nationality:** British
- **Famous books include:** *War Horse*, *Kensuke's Kingdom*, *The Butterfly Lion* and *Private Peaceful*
- **Favourite authors:** Robert Louis Stevenson, Ted Hughes and Rudyard Kipling
- **Likes:** theatre, music, film, animals and the countryside

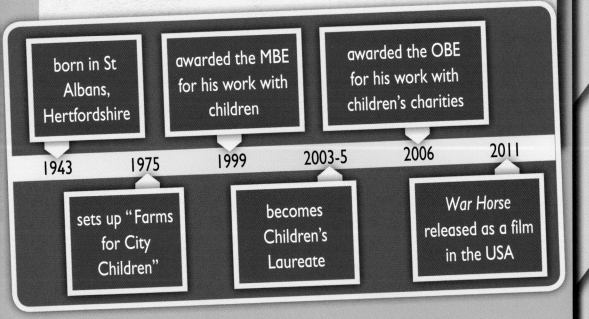

born in St Albans, Hertfordshire

awarded the MBE for his work with children

awarded the OBE for his work with children's charities

1943   1975   1999   2003-5   2006   2011

sets up "Farms for City Children"

becomes Children's Laureate

War Horse released as a film in the USA

From Pirates to Primary School

Michael Morpurgo has written more than 120 books for children. Stories have been a huge part of his life ever since he was read to as a child.

Michael didn't write much as a child, but he loved stories.

When Michael was young, his mother used to read him stories from *The Jungle Book*. One of the first books he read on his own was Robert Louis Stevenson's *Treasure Island*, the exciting tale of Jim Hawkins, who becomes a cabin boy on a pirate ship. Michael remembers feeling as if he was living the story as he read it.

Michael's father was an actor called Tony Bridge. His parents **separated** when Michael was a baby and he later took on the surname of his stepfather, Jack Morpurgo.

Sad Inspiration

Michael was sent away to boarding school. He hated it and later used some of the bad things that happened to him in *The Butterfly Lion*, when a boy runs away from the school where he is being bullied.

> **I wasn't particularly gifted with writing at school and wasn't much good at reading either ... but I loved stories.**
> Michael Morpurgo

Michael still loves to read books to children today.

Story Maker

After school, Michael joined the army but left soon afterwards to get married. Both Michael and his wife, Clare, became primary school teachers.

It was reading stories aloud to his class that led Michael to begin writing. One day his pupils were restless because the story was dull, so he made up his own tale. The children liked it so much that they didn't want to leave when the bell rang. Michael began to realise that he had a talent for writing.

Farming and Fiction

Michael's first book for children was a set of short stories called *It Never Rained*, which was published in 1974. The following year, he and his wife decided to change their lives completely when they stopped teaching and moved to Devon.

Charity Work

Michael and Clare decided to run a farm in Devon. They set up a charity called "Farms for City Children". Its purpose was to give children from inner city areas a week in the countryside, living and working on a farm. It has been a massive success: in the last 30 years over 50,000 children have benefited from it.

At "Farms for City Children", children help with all of the daily tasks on the farm.

> They learn hands-on where their food comes from, so, by the end of a week, they go back knowing what an extraordinary place the countryside is, knowing about planting, harvesting, milking, mucking out, feeding the animals, herding sheep.
>
> Michael Morpurgo

Two Supporters

In Devon, Michael met two local writers: poet Sean Rafferty (1909–98), and Ted Hughes (1930–98), who wrote the children's tale, *The Iron Man*. They encouraged Michael to keep writing. Michael also worked with Ted Hughes to write a diary of a year on the farm, which was published in 1979. This close contact with writers boosted Michael's confidence. He knew he was ready to write about more difficult subjects.

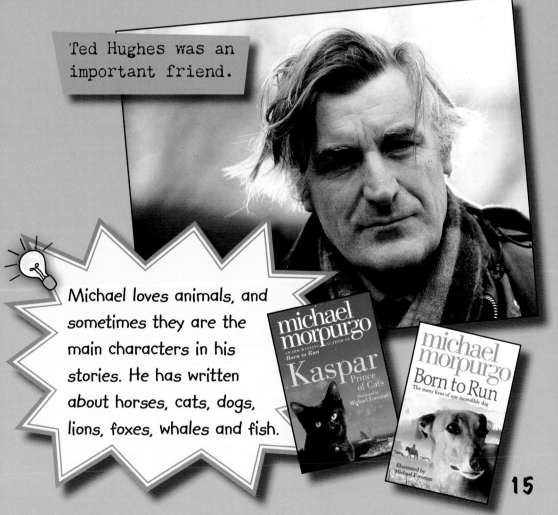

Ted Hughes was an important friend.

Michael loves animals, and sometimes they are the main characters in his stories. He has written about horses, cats, dogs, lions, foxes, whales and fish.

A Story of Suffering

It was a chance meeting that led Michael to the story that would make him famous. In his village pub one evening, Michael met an old soldier who had fought in the First World War. The old man told Michael how lots of horses were used in that war and how he used to whisper his deepest fears to them.

Horse Puppets

Michael was inspired to write *War Horse*, a story about the terrible suffering of men and horses in the First World War. The story was published in 1982 and then was made into a hugely successful play in which the horses are played by extraordinary life-sized puppets.
In 2011, the film *War Horse* was released.

The horse puppets are operated by puppeteers who control the puppets' movements using levers.

Plots and People

Michael's recent books are also winning praise. In 2011, he won the Red House Children's Book Award for his **novel** *Shadow*. It's about a boy trying to get away from war in Afghanistan, helped by the bravest dog in the world.

Michael says that putting pen to paper is the very last stage in his story making. When he has an idea, he spends months or sometimes years pondering the plot and characters. When the tale is fully planned, he finally writes it.

Michael's books are often based on real events. *Kensuke's Kingdom* was inspired by a newspaper article about a Japanese soldier who stayed on a desert island for 28 years after the end of the Second World War.

Three of Michael's books are set on the Isles of Scilly where he goes on holiday.

Anthony Horowitz

FACT FILE

- **Name**: Anthony Horowitz
- **Date of birth**: 5th April 1956
- **Nationality**: British
- **Famous books include**: the *Groosham Grange*, *Alex Rider* and *The Power of Five* **series**
- **Favourite author**: Ian Fleming (creator of the James Bond books and *Chitty Chitty Bang Bang*)
- **Likes**: scuba diving, amusement parks, travelling, France, cinema and Tintin

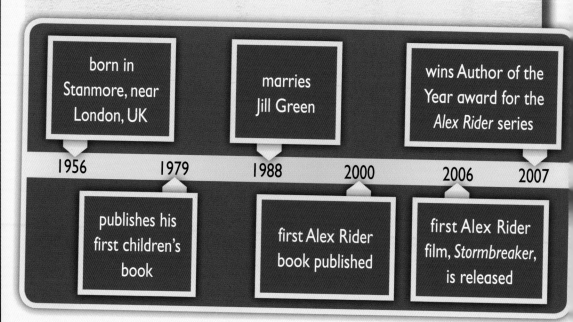

born in Stanmore, near London, UK

marries Jill Green

wins Author of the Year award for the *Alex Rider* series

1956   1979   1988   2000   2006   2007

publishes his first children's book

first Alex Rider book published

first Alex Rider film, *Stormbreaker*, is released

The Spy Master

Anthony Horowitz created the incredibly popular Alex Rider series about a teenage spy, and has written many other series and one-off books for children.

Childhood Wish

Anthony describes himself as a round and chubby child. He certainly wasn't short of food: he grew up in a rich family, with a large house, a nanny, two cooks and a chauffeur-driven Rolls Royce car. All this was paid for by his mysterious, businessman father.

As a child, Anthony desperately wanted to be a writer.

As a boy, Anthony always wanted to be an author, but none of his family thought he'd be able to make a living by writing stories.

One of Anthony's early children's stories is *Granny*, a hilarious tale about a terrible old lady. She is based on his own grandmother, whom he describes as a "monster" who bossed his family around. In the book he makes her more amusing than she really was!

Stories to Escape

Anthony went to boarding school when he was eight years old, but he had a terrible time. The staff treated him badly and the headmaster often punished pupils.

Books were Anthony's lifeline, and he began writing stories to escape from reality. As an adult he took his revenge on cruel staff by using their names for the baddies in his books! His *Groosham Grange* series about a nightmare boarding school is based on these unhappy times.

At the time Anthony was at school, teachers were allowed to punish naughty children by hitting them, usually with a **cane**, slipper or leather strap. This was called corporal punishment. It was banned in 1987 in most schools.

Anthony's mother gave him a human skull for his 13th birthday! He keeps it on his desk to remind him to work hard all his life.

Riches to Rags

When Anthony was 21 years old, his mysterious father went to Switzerland and hid his money away in a secret bank account to keep it safe. But he was already ill, and he died without telling anyone where the money was. The family fortune was lost.

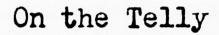

Anthony's father hid the family fortune in a secret account like this one.

On the Telly

Anthony took a job writing the text for advertisements. He was good at it, but he really wanted to write books. One wet afternoon, he wrote the first sentence of a children's book about the most unpleasant boy in the world.

The sentence grew into his first story, *The Sinister Secret of Frederick K. Bower*, which was published in 1979. Anthony then began writing scripts for TV programmes such as *Robin of Sherwood* and the *Pentagram* series, about an ancient evil that threatens the whole world. He had become an author!

The Name's Bond, Junior Bond

Over the next two decades, Anthony wrote many books and series including the **detective** series, *Diamond Brothers*, and the *Groosham Grange* series, but he wasn't really a big name in the world of children's books.

James Bond was Anthony's childhood hero.

“I used to love James Bond films, but one day it occurred to me that Bond was getting too old. It was in that single thought that Alex Rider was born.**”**
Anthony Horowitz

Action-packed

Everything changed when Anthony created the funny, action-packed Alex Rider stories, inspired by the James Bond films he loved to watch as a child. Fourteen-year-old spy Alex first appeared in *Stormbreaker*, which was published in 2000. It has sold more than nine million copies around the world, and was made into a film in 2006.

Read Me!

The *Alex Rider* books are fast-paced adventures packed with chases, shoot-ups and whacky gadgets. Anthony makes the stories as thrilling as possible, for example, by having Alex snowboard down a steep mountain on an ironing board! Gripping, non-stop suspense means the books are especially popular with boys. In 2008, Anthony won a "Champion Author" award for creating books that make boys want to read.

The Alex Rider stories are thrilling and action-packed.

Anthony found inspiration for new spy gadgets by looking at what was in his teenage sons' bedrooms. He made up devices such as plastic-explosive bubble gum or zit cream that **dissolves** metal.

A Family Business

Today Anthony is one of the busiest writers around. As well as best-selling children's books, he still writes film and TV scripts and plays. It's a family

business: his wife Jill produces some of his TV programmes, and his sons provide feedback on his writing.

Anthony's family help him to research his stories.

66 I have a note my son once gave me for a book that I had written. He said, 'Dad, there is too much description in this book. You even described what the water looks like. I know what water looks like. You know it's wet, what else is there to say?' 99
Anthony Horowitz

Sherlock Returns

Anthony says he is only totally happy when he is writing and he is always working on new ideas – and reviving some old ones. In 2011, he published *The House of Silk*, a story featuring the famous detective Sherlock Holmes. The name "Anthony Horowitz" will be on many more book covers in the future!

J. K. Rowling

FACT FILE

- **Name:** Joanne (Jo) Rowling
- **Date of birth:** 31st July 1965
- **Nationality:** British
- **Famous books:** the *Harry Potter* series
- **Favourite authors:** Jane Austen and J. R. R. Tolkien (author of fantasy story *Lord of the Rings*)
- **Likes:** sketching and playing the guitar

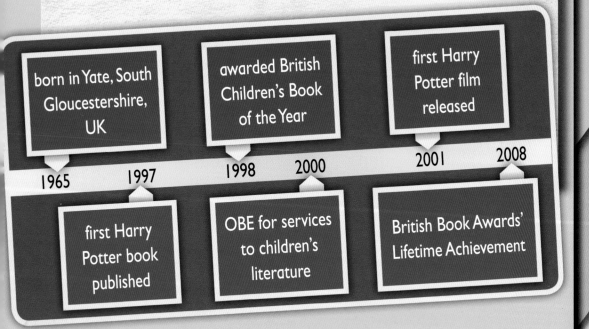

born in Yate, South Gloucestershire, UK

awarded British Children's Book of the Year

first Harry Potter film released

1965   1997   1998   2000   2001   2008

first Harry Potter book published

OBE for services to children's literature

British Book Awards' Lifetime Achievement

Stories and a Scar

Jo's earliest memory is the birth of her sister Di, when she was nearly two years old. Like many sisters, they were the best of friends except when they were fighting. Jo once hurled a battery at Di and it made a small scar just above her eyebrow. Her best-known character, Harry Potter, has a scar on his forehead, too.

Emma Watson plays Hermione Granger in the Harry Potter films.

Acting Up

Jo has said that the character of clever, book-loving Hermione is based on herself at the age of 11. She was already a keen story-teller, and she and her sister would act out the tales she dreamed up.

At birth, Jo's name was Joanne Rowling. A publisher said more boys would read her books if she changed it, so she added her grandmother's name, Kathleen, and became J. K. Rowling.

You Can Do it!

At secondary school, Jo met Sean Harris, who owned a car like the one that flies in *The Chamber of Secrets* – a book that she **dedicated** to him. He was a good friend and the only person at the time who believed Jo would become a successful writer.

The famous flying car was based on her friend's Ford Anglia.

Work and Writing

Jo studied French at Exeter University. She finished her degree in 1987 and then moved to London, where she worked at a few different office jobs. She wrote all the time, creating two novels for adults that have never been published. In 1990, Jo was on a long train journey when she suddenly had an idea for the character of a boy who doesn't know he has magic skills until he is invited to wizard school.

> I had been writing almost continuously since the age of six but I had never been so excited about an idea before.
> J. K. Rowling

The Struggle

Just after Christmas 1990, tragedy struck the Rowling family when Jo's mother died from **multiple sclerosis (MS)** at the age of 45. Jo was devastated. Needing to get away, she took a job teaching English in Portugal. Here she met and married Jorge Arantes in 1992 and they had a daughter called Jessica.

Jo and Jorge were not happy together so Jo came back to Britain to live in Edinburgh. She brought with her the huge pile of notes she had built up since 1990 for a series of seven Harry Potter books.

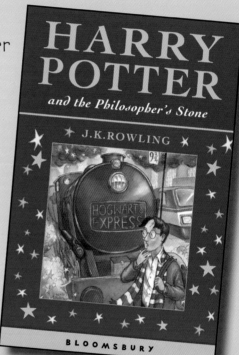

Jo always meant Harry Potter to be a series of seven books.

Jo scribbled the names of the houses in Hogwarts on to the only paper she could find at the time – an aeroplane sick bag!

Classrooms and Cafes

Jo was short of money, but she was still determined to be a writer and continued **drafting** the first Harry Potter book. Sometimes she left her cold, dingy flat and sat in a cafe to keep warm, writing while Jessica slept in her pushchair.

Jo used to write in cafes in Edinburgh where she lived.

Wizard Progress

By 1995, the book was finished and Jo sent it to **agents** in London. She was lucky: the second agent agreed to try to get it published. Twelve publishers turned down the story of the boy wizard, but in August 1996, Bloomsbury agreed to publish her book. Harry Potter was about to meet the world!

Most publishers can't cope with the huge number of stories they receive so they rely on agents to suggest the best ones. Getting an agent helps a writer to get their book noticed by publishers.

A World Superstar

The magic moment that launched J. K. Rowling as a top international author was when the American publisher, Scholastic Press, loved her book and offered $105 000 (about £66 000) to publish it in the USA. This was a massive deal for an author with no previous books to her name.

Harry Potter got a wizard response, selling well and winning many prizes. Over the next ten years, Jo worked from her careful notes to write the rest of the series. The magical saga was made into eight **blockbuster** films, with lots of spin-off toys and games. There is even a theme park named after Harry!

Children can step inside Jo's stories at a Harry Potter theme park!

> **❝** I knew how difficult it would be just to get a book published. I was a completely unknown writer. I certainly could never have expected what's happened. It's been a real shock. **❞**
> J. K. Rowling

International Celebrity

Jo is now a global superstar, and one of the wealthiest writers in the world. She uses her fame and wealth to support many charities, including those that help single mothers and sufferers of MS, the disease that killed her mother.

Jo still loves writing and working on new projects. In 2011, she launched "Pottermore", a website packed with background information on the Harry Potter books.

Jo attends movie premieres and book signings. She is pictured with her second husband, Neil Murray.

Millions of children around the world can't wait to find out what she is going to publish next.

Glossary

agents people who help authors to get their books published

attaché someone who works abroad for the government

blockbuster very popular film

cane rod made of thin wood

dedicated mentioned a special person in the front of a book

detective someone who tries to solve crimes

dissolves mixes a solid into a liquid

drafting creating a first piece of writing

gobstoppers large round sweets

multiple sclerosis (MS) disease that makes it difficult to control your body

novel long story book

permanent lasts for ever

plot events that happen in a story

separated decided to live apart

series set of books or TV programmes that have some of the same features or characters

traditional something that has been known or done for many years

Index